UNLEASH THE POWER OF WUKONG

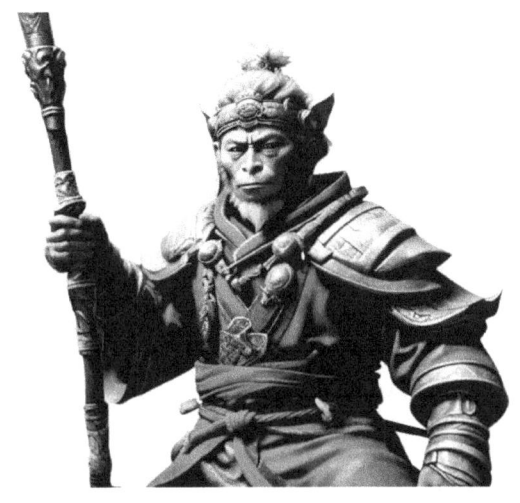

A Black Myth: Wukong Game Guide and Strategy Book.

RYAN W. PEREZ

Copyright © Ryan W. Perez, 2024

All rights reserved. No part of this book may be reproduced, distributed, or transmitted in any form or by any means, including photocopying, recording, or other electronic or mechanical methods, without the prior written permission of the author or publisher, except in the case of brief quotations embodied in critical reviews and certain other noncommercial uses permitted by copyright law.

Disclaimer

This book, "A Black Myth: Wukong Game Guide and Strategy Book" is an unofficial guide and is not endorsed by or affiliated with the creators or original copyright holders of " Black Myth"

The strategies, tips, and secrets discussed in this guide are the author's interpretations and personal insights into the game and are intended to help enhance the gaming experience for players.

Table of Contents

INTRODUCTION..7
  Welcome to the Mythical World of Wukong.....................7
  About This Guide: Making the Most of Your Journey.... 10
  A Quick Overview of "Black Myth: Wukong"................. 13
CHAPTER 1.. 18
  Understanding the Legend..18
  The Story Behind Black Myth: Wukong.......................... 18
  Who is Sun Wukong? Exploring Myth and Game.......... 21
  Key Themes and Inspirations in Journey to the West..... 23
CHAPTER 2.. 28
  Getting Started..28
  System Requirements and Setup...................................... 28
  Navigating the User Interface...31
  Basic controls and game mechanics................................. 34
CHAPTER 3.. 38
  The Art of Battle: Combat Mechanics and Strategies..... 38
  Weapons and Upgrades: Selecting the Best Gear............42
  Magical Abilities: Utilizing Wukong's Powers............... 45
  Combinations and Special Moves: Performing Flawless Attacks... 47
CHAPTER 4.. 51
  Exploring the World... 51
  Regions and Environments: A Guide to the Game's

    Landscape 51
    Hidden Secrets and Easter Eggs 54
    Navigating quests and side missions 57
CHAPTER 5 61
    Boss Battles 61
    Facing the most formidable foes 62
    Understanding Boss' Patterns and Weaknesses 63
    Winning Strategies for Each Major Battle 65
    General Tips for Boss Battles 70
CHAPTER 6 72
    Character Progression 72
    Leveling Up: How to Improve Wukong's Abilities 73
    Developing the Ultimate Skill Set 74
    Manage Resources: Health, Mana, and More 76
    Balancing Resource Management and Combat Strategy . 78
CHAPTER 7 82
    Advanced Tactics 82
    Expert Tips for Combat Mastery 83
    Shapeshifting: Using Wukong's Transformations 85
    Adapting Strategies to Different Playstyles 87
CHAPTER 8 92
    Crafting and Resources 92
    Upgrade Weapons and Armor 95
    Balancing crafting and combat 99
CHAPTER 9 101
    Multiplayer and Community 101
    Join the Black Myth Community 104
    Balancing Multiplayer and Solo Play 109
CHAPTER 10 111

Troubleshooting and FAQs... 111
Common Issues and Solutions..112
Frequently Asked Questions...116
CHAPTER 11... **123**
The Future of Black Myth: Wukong.............................. 123
What to Expect in the Future of the Game..................... 126
Engaging with the Game's Future...................................130
APPENDICES.. **138**

INTRODUCTION

Welcome to the Mythical World of Wukong

Imagine a world where legends come to life, ancient tales unfold amid gorgeous scenery, and you, the player, have the ability to alter the fate of a famous hero. Welcome to the intriguing realm of Black Myth: Wukong, a game that combines mythical storyline with cutting-edge gameplay to offer an experience unlike any other.

Sun Wukong, the legendary Monkey King, is at the center of this quest, and his stories have been handed down through centuries in Chinese mythology. Sun Wukong has captivated audiences for ages with his power, humor, and rebellious attitude, and now you can put yourself in his shoes and go on an epic quest.

In Black Myth: Wukong, you'll find yourself immersed in a world full of mysterious creatures, tough opponents, and breathtaking scenery. From lush woods and towering mountains to ancient temples and heavenly worlds, the game's graphics transport you to a world where every turn leads to a new adventure and every obstacle tests your abilities.

As you explore this fantastical environment, you'll come across a diverse cast of individuals, each with their own story and objectives. Allies will assist you in your journey, while foes will test your strength and ingenuity. The game's storyline combines aspects of fantasy, action, and strategy, ensuring that each moment is both interesting and rewarding.

Whether you're interested in the game's complicated battle system, engaging plot, or gorgeous graphics, Black Myth: Wukong promises an exciting journey that will have you on the edge of your seat. This planet is waiting for you to discover its mysteries and unleash the might of Wukong.

About This Guide: Making the Most of Your Journey.

This handbook is your reliable companion as you go through the realm of Black Myth: Wukong. Whether you're a seasoned player aiming to master every facet of the game or a newbie searching for advice on your first playing, this book is intended to give essential insights, tips, and techniques to improve your gaming experience.

In the coming chapters, we'll go deep into the game's mechanics, covering everything from battle methods and character growth to exploring the enormous environment and discovering hidden treasures. Our goal is to provide you with the information and skills necessary to face any challenge and emerge successful.

Each chapter is designed to be accessible to players of all skill levels, providing step-by-step instructions, thorough explanations, and practical tips to help you explore the game with confidence. We'll go over the fundamentals for those who are new to Black Myth: Wukong, as well as advanced tactics and strategies for veteran players who want to improve their skills.

This tutorial is more than simply teaching you how to play the game; it also empowers you to be the hero of your own journey. By the end of the book, you'll have a thorough comprehension of the game's mechanics, an appreciation for its complex story, and the ability to plan effectively, allowing you to easily overcome any problem.

Whether you want to learn battle methods, discover secret locations, or just enjoy the tale at your own speed, this guide will help you every step of the way. We'll go on a voyage into the mythological kingdom of Wukong, unravelling its secrets and finding the true might of the Monkey King.

A Quick Overview of "Black Myth: Wukong"

Black Myth: Wukong is a breakthrough action role-playing game created by the creative team at Game Science. Drawing inspiration from the legendary narrative of Journey to the West, the game provides a unique and immersive perspective on the traditional story, allowing players to experience Sun Wukong's exploits in a whole new manner.

The game's story is strongly founded in Chinese mythology, bringing to life legendary people and exotic animals that have captivated audiences for years. As Sun Wukong, you'll go on a heroic mission to defeat monsters, explore mysterious worlds, and unearth the universe's mysteries.

Black Myth: Wukong is fundamentally a game of skill and strategy. The fighting system is intended to be both tough and rewarding, requiring players to learn a wide range of tactics and skills in order to overcome their opponents. From completing devastating combinations to harnessing magical powers, the game provides a wide variety of options for customizing your playstyle and adapting to every circumstance.

One of the game's most notable aspects is its dynamic and interactive settings. The universe of Black Myth: Wukong is rich in detail, with several possibilities for exploration and discovery. From hidden riches and secret passageways to epic boss fights and story-driven missions, every instant presents a chance to interact with the environment and discover its secrets.

As you continue through the game, you will be able to improve Wukong's powers by modifying his talents and traits to fit your chosen playstyle. The advancement mechanism is intended to be both versatile and rewarding, enabling you to experiment with various techniques and create the best version of Sun Wukong.

In addition to its captivating gameplay and story, Black Myth: Wukong is known for its outstanding graphics and art design. The game's settings demonstrate the development team's creativity and devotion, as they have built a world that is both gorgeous and immersive. Every environment, character, and monster is meticulously designed, bringing the mythological realm of Wukong to life in breathtaking form.

Whether you like action RPGs, are interested in mythology, or are just searching for a new adventure, Black Myth: Wukong provides a tough and satisfying experience. The game's compelling plot, inventive gameplay, and magnificent graphics promise to fascinate and leave a lasting impression.

This guide will help you uncover the full potential of Black Myth: Wukong by giving you the tools and information you need to overcome the game's difficulties and reach mastery. Whether you want to beat every boss, discover every secret, or just enjoy the adventure, this guide is here to help.

Join us as we explore the mysterious land of Wukong, solving its secrets and finding the Monkey King's true might. Together, we'll go on an expedition that promises to be both fascinating and informative, unlocking the mysteries of a game that has captivated audiences all over the globe.

CHAPTER 1

Understanding the Legend

The Story Behind Black Myth: Wukong

Every epic quest starts with a tale, and Black Myth: Wukong is no different. This game is inspired by Journey to the West, one of Chinese literature's most famous masterpieces. This story, written by Wu Cheng'en during the Ming Dynasty, has captivated readers for centuries with its combination of mythology, adventure, and moral precept

At the centre of Black Myth: Wukong lies the fabled Monkey King, Sun Wukong, a man whose deeds and personality have made him a cultural symbol. The game reimagines this old narrative through the prism of current gaming, allowing players to see the magnitude of his epic achievements firsthand.

In Black Myth: Wukong, players are immersed in a gorgeously portrayed universe that blends classic mythology with spectacular visual features and cutting-edge gameplay. The game builds on the original story, offering a new viewpoint on the Monkey King's quest. You'll not only see but also participate in the experiences that have fashioned Wukong's mythology. This reinterpretation not only brings the narrative to life, but it also allows you to participate by engaging with the people and situations that have long captivated the imagination.

Who is Sun Wukong? Exploring Myth and Game

Sun Wukong, commonly referred to as the Monkey King, is a character of enormous power and charm. In traditional mythology, he is a rebellious and ferociously intelligent monkey born from stone who transforms into a fearsome force via hard training and the development of magical talents. His persona combines power, cunning, and a hint of mischief, making him a popular figure in Chinese culture.

Wukong's quest is about self-discovery and redemption. After opposing the heavenly order and spreading havoc in the sky, he is finally humbled and gains enlightenment with the help of a Buddhist monk. His tale revolves on the struggle for redemption and spiritual progress, which reflects themes of change and inner serenity.

In Black Myth: Wukong, gamers may walk into Wukong's footsteps and explore his realm in unparalleled detail. The game lets you experience his powers and skills firsthand, from his distinctive staff, which may grow to enormous proportions, to his magical transformations. Wukong's mobility and martial talents are at your disposal, resulting in a dynamic and compelling gaming experience that replicates his legendary achievements.

As you go through the game, you will meet a variety of characters and face difficulties that mirror important parts of Wukong's narrative. His encounters with gods, devils, and other legendary creatures are brought to life via breathtaking visuals and sophisticated storyline. This comprehensive experience enables you to dive further into his personality and comprehend the complexity of his legacy.

Key Themes and Inspirations in Journey to the West

Journey to the West is a complex tapestry of concepts and philosophical ideas, not merely an action novel. The work delves into themes such as loyalty, redemption, and the desire for enlightenment. These concepts are effortlessly integrated into Black Myth: Wukong, strengthening the game's storyline and giving players a better grasp of the original material.

One of the key themes of Journey to the West is the concept of personal change. Wukong's transformation from a rebellious trickster to a disciplined and enlightened creature exemplifies the larger topic of self-improvement and spiritual development. This notion is represented in the game's mechanics, which require players to improve their talents and abilities in order to conquer obstacles and grow as characters.

Another major topic is the balance between chaos and order. Wukong's initial disobedience of the cosmic order and subsequent quest for forgiveness emphasize the conflict between these conflicting powers. This notion is reflected in Black Myth: Wukong's complex fighting system and complicated stories, which require players to manage conflicts and strike a balance in their actions.

The game is also inspired by the rich visuals and symbolism of Journey to the West. The different environments, which range from lush woods to towering mountains, are more than simply backgrounds; they are vital to the plot and gameplay. These landscapes echo the novel's mysterious and mythical qualities, creating a universe that is both captivating and vibrant.

Furthermore, the game contains aspects of ancient Chinese culture and mythology, paying tribute to the original material while also adding a contemporary spin. This combination of old and modern provides a one-of-a-kind gaming experience that pays homage to the heritage of Journey to the West while still giving a fresh and exciting journey.

In conclusion, Black Myth: Wukong is a brilliant reworking of a classic mythology. By combining Journey to the West's rich narrative and concepts with unique gameplay and breathtaking graphics, the game provides an immersive experience that brings Sun Wukong's tale to life in a fresh and thrilling manner. As you begin on this trip, you will not only discover the magical kingdom of Wukong, but also develop a greater understanding of the mythology that has inspired generations.

CHAPTER 2

Getting Started

System Requirements and Setup

Before plunging into the captivating world of Black Myth: Wukong, be sure your gaming equipment is up to the challenge. Understanding the system requirements and setting your setup will guarantee a seamless and immersive experience from the start.

System Requirements: Black Myth: Wukong is a graphically spectacular game that requires a specific degree of hardware performance to fully realize its potential. Here's a brief breakdown of the required system specs to get you started:

- Operating System: Windows 10 (64-bit) or newer
- Processor: AMD Ryzen 7 3700X or Intel Core i7-9700K.
- Memory: 16 GB RAM.
- GPU: NVIDIA GeForce RTX 2080 or AMD Radeon RX 5700 XT.
- DirectX: Version 12 - Storage: 50 GB available

These parameters guarantee that you may enjoy the game's detailed visuals and complicated dynamics without any performance issues. If your system meets or exceeds these specifications, you're ready for adventure. If not, you should consider updating your hardware to fully enjoy the game's stunning graphics and smooth gameplay.

Setup and Installation: After you've checked that your system is ready, follow these instructions to install Black Myth: Wukong.

1. Buy and download the game from your choice digital or physical vendor. To minimize disruptions during downloading, verify that you have a reliable internet connection.
2. Run the installation: Locate the downloaded file and launch the installation. Follow the on-screen directions to install the game on your desired drive.
3. Update the Game: Once installed, check for any updates or patches. Developers often

provide updates to address problems and improve performance.

4. Configure Settings: Launch the game and go to the settings menu to customize the visuals, audio, and controls to your tastes and system capabilities.

With everything in place, you're ready to go on your voyage through the magical land of Wukong!

Navigating the User Interface

Understanding the user interface (UI) is critical to a smooth gaming experience. The interface of Black Myth: Wukong is intended to be intuitive, with quick access to major functions and information. Here's an overview of the major components you'll encounter:

- **Main Menu:** When you start the game, you will be met with the main menu. This is where you may start a new game, load a saved game, change your settings, or leave the game. The primary menu is simple, with clearly labeled choices for quick navigating.

- **In-Game HUD (Heads-Up Display):** During gameplay, your HUD displays important information like health, mana, and mission objectives. Here's what you should look for:

- **Health and Mana bars:** These bars, which are often positioned in the top-left or bottom-left corners of the screen, display your current health and mana levels. Keeping an eye on these is critical for survival and successful fighting.

 - **Mini Map**: The mini-map, which is usually located in the top-right corner, helps you traverse the game environment. It displays your location, neighboring areas of interest, and quest markers.

 - **Ability and Item spaces:** These spaces are at the bottom of the screen and show your active abilities and items. You can rapidly access and utilize them while fighting or exploring.

- **Menu Navigation:** To access complex menus like inventory, skills, and missions, use the appropriate buttons or hotkeys. Familiarize yourself with these choices so you can effectively control your character and progress.

Navigating the universe: The game's universe is huge and full of interactive features. Use the mini-map and in-game cues to get to key locales, quest objectives, and hidden mysteries. Pay close attention to environmental signals and NPC interaction to discover new places and tales.

Basic controls and game mechanics

Mastering the fundamental controls and gameplay concepts is required to truly appreciate Black Myth: Wukong. Here is a tutorial to help you get started.

- **Movement:** To move Wukong about the game environment, use your keyboard's WASD buttons or your controller's left analog stick. Practice using these controls to explore different terrains and avoid hazards.

- **Combat:** Combat is an essential component of Black Myth: Wukong. Here is how to start:

 - **Attacking:** To conduct basic attacks, use the left mouse button or the right trigger on your controller. Combine them with the right mouse button or left trigger to perform unique attacks or abilities.

- **Dodging and blocking:** Use the spacebar or a specific button to avoid opposing strikes. Blocking may be done with the right mouse button or a particular button on your controller, depending on your configuration.

- **Special skills**: Wukong has special skills that may be used with the number keys or face buttons on your controller. Experiment with various abilities to see which ones fit your playstyle.

- **Interacting with Objects:** To interact with objects, NPCs, or quest items, approach them and press the 'E' key or the appropriate button on your gamepad. This allows you to pick up things, initiate discussions, and activate events.

- **Inventory Management:** To access your inventory, hit 'I' or the corresponding button. You may see and equip things here, as well as manage your resources and check your mission log. Check your inventory on a regular basis to ensure that you have all of your equipment and supplies.

- **Exploration:** The realm of Black Myth: Wukong is full with mysteries and hidden riches. Take your time exploring various places, interacting with NPCs, and completing side missions to improve your gaming experience.

Tips for Success: - Practice basic controls and fighting methods to improve skills and confidence.

- **Explore Thoroughly:** Do not speed through the game. Explore every corner and crevice to find hidden treasures and mysteries.
- **Adapt to Challenges:** Each adversary and boss has distinct dynamics. Adapt your methods to the obstacles you confront.

With these fundamentals in hand, you're ready to go on your journey in Black Myth: Wukong. As you go through the game, you'll discover new mechanics, mysteries, and methods that will help you on your adventure. Happy gaming!

CHAPTER 3

The Art of Battle: Combat Mechanics and Strategies

Combat in Black Myth: Wukong is more than simply a reflex test; it's a dynamic ballet that requires strategy, timing, and talent. Understanding the fundamental physics and implementing smart methods might be the difference between a successful encounter and a devastating loss.

1. Combat mechanics: Black Myth: Wukong's fighting system is primarily intended to be fluid and responsive. Here's a rundown of the main mechanics you'll need to master:

- Basic Attacks: These are the fundamental methods of delivering damage. To increase your offense, combine mild and heavy assaults. Light attacks are faster and allow for more frequent blows, while heavy attacks deliver more damage but take longer to complete.

- Dodging and Blocking: Dodging is necessary to dodge opposing strikes. Use the dodge mechanism to swiftly avoid attacks and reposition yourself. Blocking, on the other hand, allows you to absorb attack damage and avoid absorbing complete blows. Mastering the timing of your dodges and blocks is crucial for surviving more difficult bouts.

- Adversary Patterns: Every adversary in Black Myth: Wukong has a distinct assault style and behavior. Pay attention to these patterns so that you may predict and counter their movements successfully. Look for visual and aural clues indicating oncoming strikes or special maneuvers.

2. Combat techniques: Using successful techniques may swing the tide of combat in your favor. Here are some pointers to help you succeed:

- Use Terrain to Your Advantage: The environment may have a huge impact on fighting. Utilize barriers, elevation, and space to navigate and establish favorable positions. For example, utilizing high ground might provide you a greater view position and make it simpler to evade hostile strikes.

- Prioritize Targets: In confrontations with several foes, prioritize your targets according to threat level. Take down adversaries that offer the most imminent threat first, such as those with strong ranged attacks or healing skills.

- Adapt Your Approach: Be prepared to change your tactics depending on the sort of foes you're up against. For example, some adversaries may be more vulnerable to certain sorts of assaults or elemental harm. To take advantage of their shortcomings, adjust your methods appropriately.

Weapons and Upgrades: Selecting the Best Gear

In Black Myth: Wukong, the proper equipment may substantially improve your fighting efficiency. Understanding the various weapons and upgrades available will allow you to customize your kit for your playstyle and the obstacles you encounter.

1. Weapon Types: Wukong may use a number of weapons, each with its own set of traits and benefits. Here's an overview of some of the primary weapon types:

- Staff: Wukong's signature weapon, the staff, is both flexible and strong. It may be expanded to allow for both melee and distance strikes.

Upgrading the staff allows it to do more damage and get access to new powers.

- Melee Weapons: These are swords, axes, and other close-combat weapons. Each has unique attack patterns and damage characteristics. Choose melee weapons that suit your fighting style, whether you favor fast blows or hefty hits.

- Ranged Weapons: Ranged weapons enable you to strike from afar, which may be handy when dealing with foes that like to maintain their distance. Ranged weapons such as bows and magical projectiles may be modified to boost their efficacy.

2. Upgrades and Customization: Upgrading your weapons and gear is critical for keeping an advantage in battle. Here's how to handle upgrades:

- Weapon Upgrades: Invest in upgrades to improve your weapon's damage, speed, and special effects. Look for resources and crafting alternatives that will boost the performance of your weapons.

- Armor and Accessories: In addition to weapons, armor and accessories are quite important in battle. Equip goods that give more protection, boost your attacking powers, or provide special perks. Customizing your gear to fit your playstyle may have a huge impact in combat.

Magical Abilities: Utilizing Wukong's Powers

Wukong's magical powers are the foundation of his fighting ability. Mastering these abilities may give you a substantial edge in combat and enable you to unleash deadly blows on your opponents.

1. Understanding powers: Wukong's magical powers include a wide spectrum of strong skills and spells. Here are some of the main talents you should master:

- Transformation: Wukong is capable of transforming into a variety of beasts, each with its own set of powers. Use transformations to acquire tactical benefits in battle, such as greater strength or agility.

- Elemental Powers: Elemental powers may inflict substantial harm on foes and exploit their vulnerabilities. Mastering these talents enables you to adapt to various battle scenarios and improves your attacking capabilities.

- Healing and Support: Some magical powers are centered on healing and support. Use these abilities to replenish health, strengthen your defenses, or deliver other advantages that may tip the balance of combat.

2. Ability Upgrades: Improving Wukong's skills is critical to increasing their usefulness. Focus on strengthening your basic powers and unlocking additional ones to expand your battle choices. Experiment with various ability combinations to see which ones best fit your playstyle.

Combinations and Special Moves: Performing Flawless Attacks

Executing combinations and special attacks correctly may dramatically enhance your damage output while making fight more dynamic and fun.

1. Mastering Combos: Combos are a series of strikes that, when done properly, cause greater damage and stun or incapacitate opponents. Chain mild and heavy blows to form formidable combinations. Timing and accuracy are essential for completing these combinations properly.

2. Special Moves: Special moves are strong assaults or skills that may change the course of a fight. These maneuvers often need particular circumstances or resources to function. Learn how to trigger and use special maneuvers for maximum effect. Combining them with your usual assaults has catastrophic consequences.

3. Practice and accuracy: Understanding combinations and special techniques need practice and accuracy. Spend time in combat training areas or against weaker opponents to hone your skills and enhance your timing.

Tips For Combat Success:

- Stay Mobile: Constant mobility allows you to evade opposing strikes and position yourself strategically.

- Study adversary habits and assault patterns in order to predict and counter their movements effectively.
- Use skills Wisely: Make sure your magical skills and special moves are accessible when you need them the most.

With these methods and insights, you'll be well prepared to conquer battle in Black Myth: Wukong. Whether you're fighting ferocious adversaries, exploring exotic regions, or learning hidden mysteries, efficient combat skills will be your ticket to victory. Accept the challenge, refine your abilities, and unleash Wukong's full might as you begin on your epic journey.

CHAPTER 4

Exploring the World

Regions and Environments: A Guide to the Game's Landscape

The realm of Black Myth: Wukong is a vast and varied area with stunning scenery. Exploring these locations entails more than simply navigating the map; it's about immersing oneself in a live, breathing universe inspired by myth and imagination. Here's a guide to navigating and enjoying the game's varied environments.

1. Diverse Regions: Each place in Black Myth: Wukong has a distinct mood and set of obstacles. Here are some of the important locations you may encounter:

- Mystical Forests: These lush, green landscapes are filled with wildlife and hidden perils. The lush vegetation and tall trees create a maze-like environment that encourages cautious exploration. Look for hidden roads and secret groves that might lead to rare treasures or fascinating side quests.

- Ancient Ruins: These ruins, found across the game environment, provide a look into the past. They are often host to powerful treasures and lost legends. As you explore these collapsing ruins, be prepared to confront ancient guardians and solve enigmatic riddles.

- Celestial Peaks: High above the clouds, the Celestial Peaks provide breathtaking views and tough terrain. The thin air and precipitous cliffs make this area both beautiful and dangerous. Explore the heights to discover hidden tunnels and ancient shrines containing great mysteries.

- Dark Caves and Dungeons: These subterranean labyrinths are fraught with peril and intrigue. With their gloomy illumination and twisting corridors, they are ideal for those looking for a challenge. Look for secret rooms and unique objects in the game's darkest regions.

2. Environmental Interactions: The game's surroundings are intended to be interactive and dynamic. Here's how to make use of them:

- Environmental risks include traps, pitfalls, and dangerous creatures. Use your environment to your advantage by enticing adversaries into traps or manipulating barriers to hide.

- Dynamic Weather and Time of Day: The game has a dynamic weather system and shifting times of day, which might impact gameplay. Rain, fog, and other meteorological conditions may affect vision and fighting efficiency. Use these elements to your advantage, or adjust your strategy as necessary.

Hidden Secrets and Easter Eggs

One of the most enjoyable aspects of exploring Black Myth: Wukong is discovering its many hidden mysteries and Easter eggs. These surprises add dimension to the game and reward players' curiosity and perseverance. Here's a guide for discovering some of the game's best-kept secrets:

1. Secret spots: Throughout the game environment, there are secret spots that are off the main road. These regions often include uncommon goods, strong artifacts, or unique encounters. To discover them, look for subtle indications and contextual cues such as unique marks or concealed doorways.

2. Easter Eggs: The makers of Black Myth: Wukong added various Easter eggs as a gesture to fans and to offer another layer of pleasure to the game. These may include allusions to other games and media, as well as hilarious encounters with NPCs. Keep an eye out for unusual elements and hidden meanings that may not be immediately obvious.

3. Hidden Challenges: Certain mysteries are associated with unique challenges or mini-games. These challenges may include solving riddles, fighting formidable opponents, or accomplishing certain tasks within a set time frame. Completing these tasks typically earns you rare goodies or awards.

4. Interactions with NPCs: Non-player characters (NPCs) often have their own storylines and mysteries. Engage in chats with them to discover secret quests, lore, or side objectives. Some NPCs may give helpful tips or information as to where to uncover hidden secrets.

Navigating quests and side missions

Quests and side missions are essential components of Black Myth: Wukong's gameplay. They allow you to explore the universe, develop your character, and discover new elements of the plot. Here's how to navigate and get the most out of these quests:

1. Primary Quests: The primary quests drive the game's basic plot. Follow these missions to advance through the tale and see important events and discoveries. To keep on track, follow the quest markers and goals.

2. Side Missions: These missions provide extra substance and opportunity for exploration. These tasks might range from assisting NPCs with personal objectives to completing environmental challenges. Completing side tasks may lead to important prizes and a better grasp of the game universe.

3. Quest Log and Tracking: Use the quest log to keep track of your current goals and objectives. The journal contains specific information on your quests, such as goals, locations, and prizes. Check it on a frequent basis to keep organized and avoid forgetting about crucial activities.

4. Choosing tasks: Certain side tasks may be more difficult or lucrative than others. Select tasks depending on your current skill level, equipment, and hobbies. If you're seeking for a certain prize or experience, choose missions that match your objectives.

5. Rewards and Progression: Completing quests and side tasks earns you numerous rewards, including experience points, goods, and improvements. Use these gifts to improve your character and equipment. Furthermore, some objectives may unlock additional locations or features in the game.

Tips For Effective Exploration:

- Explore Thoroughly: Take your time exploring each area and engaging with your surroundings. You never know what mysteries or riches you may unearth.
- Use map markers. Mark essential spots on your map for easier navigation and to avoid missing vital regions or goals.

- Stay interested: Keep an open mind and be interested about anything you come across. The most satisfying discoveries often come from unexpected places.

With this guide, you'll be well-prepared to explore the vast universe of Black Myth: Wukong. Whether you're discovering hidden mysteries, exploring varied settings, or completing tasks, every facet of the game provides a distinct and entertaining experience. Accept the journey and let your curiosity guide you to fresh discoveries in this fantastic universe.

CHAPTER 5

Boss Battles

In Black Myth: Wukong, boss fights are the height of difficulty and excitement. These encounters will put your abilities, strategy, and endurance to the test. Each monster is a distinct and tough opponent that need more than physical might to beat. To succeed, you must grasp their tendencies, exploit their flaws, and adjust your strategies. Here's a thorough guide to helping you overcome these tremendous problems.

Facing the most formidable foes

Boss confrontations in Black Myth: Wukong are intended to be unique experiences, mixing intense fighting with complicated gameplay. These bosses are often essential to the game's plot, serving as significant challenges in your path. Each boss encounter is unique, necessitating distinct methods and approaches.

1. Preparation is Essential: Before approaching a manager, make sure you are well-prepared. This involves having the proper equipment, enough healing supplies, and knowledge of the boss's skills. Equip gear that boosts your abilities and counters the boss's most devastating assaults.

2. Analyzing the Boss' powers: Bosses possess a variety of powers that make them tough opponents. These may include deadly area-of-effect assaults, tremendous melee blows, or summoning new adversaries. Take notice of these talents and develop effective counter-strategies.

Understanding Boss' Patterns and Weaknesses

Each monster in Black Myth: Wukong has a unique attack style and vulnerabilities. Recognizing and using them may transform an apparently enormous task into a manageable one.

1. Recognize Attack Patterns: Bosses often use certain attack sequences or patterns. Pay close attention to these patterns so that you can predict their movements and react appropriately. For example, a boss may launch a devastating ranged assault before closing in for melee attacks. Identifying these patterns allows you to prepare to dodge or block successfully.

2. Capitalize on Weaknesses: Bosses have flaws that can be exploited to your advantage. These flaws may be linked to certain stages of the battle or kinds of strikes. For example, a monster with thick armor plate may be susceptible to elemental damage or certain weapons. Experiment with several ways to see what works best.

3. Take Advantage of Environmental Features: The fight arena often includes environmental aspects that you may utilize to your advantage. This might contain cover locations, dangers that could hurt the boss, or vantage positions from which to attack. Use these components wisely to get an advantage in the battle.

Winning Strategies for Each Major Battle.

1. First Major Battle: The Stone Guardian

The Stone Guardian is a massive, rock-based monster with incredible physical strength and a variety of devastating ground-shaking assaults.

To overcome this dangerous monster, you must rely on agility and timing.

- Dodge and Weave: The Guardian's ground assaults may generate large shockwaves that do substantial damage. Stay mobile and make rapid dodges to evade these shockwaves. Watch for visual indications that indicate when the Guardian is ready to strike.

- Target Weak areas: The Guardian has a number of weak areas on its back and legs. Concentrate your assaults on these places to cause extra damage. Use ranged attacks or abilities that enable you to target certain areas while remaining beyond of the Guardian's grasp.

- Use the Arena: The fight arena has many elevated platforms that may protect you from the

Guardian's strikes. Use these platforms to your advantage, preparing for strikes while avoiding ground-based shockwaves.

2. Second Major Battle: The Celestial Dragon

The Celestial Dragon is a gorgeous yet frightening monster that uses strong breath attacks and aerial moves. Defeating this monster demands a combination of quickness and intelligent timing.

- Beware of Breath strikes: The Dragon's breath strikes span a large area and may cause significant damage. To avoid getting caught in the Dragon's strike, keep an eye out for its charging motion and timing your dodges correctly.

- Attack During Quiet Moments: The Dragon periodically rests on the ground to gather its breath. Use these times to inflict tremendous damage, concentrating on the Dragon's head and wings for maximum effect.

- Use High Ground: The Dragon's aerial assaults are difficult to dodge from the ground. Use high terrain or higher platforms to have a better view position and dodge Dragon's breath assaults.

3. Third Major Battle: The Abyssal Warden

The Abyssal Warden is a dark, malicious entity with formidable black magic and summoning skills. To deal with this boss's summoning and magical assaults, you must proceed with caution.

- Manage Summoned opponents: The Warden has the ability to call extra opponents throughout the conflict. To prevent being overwhelmed, focus on removing these minions as rapidly as possible. Use area-of-effect attacks or abilities to effectively handle large groups of adversaries.

- Counter Magic strikes: The Warden's magical strikes may be very damaging. Use blocking and evading methods to reduce the damage caused by these assaults. Pay attention to the Warden's casting motions to predict and counter its spells.

- Take Advantage of Vulnerability Phases: The Warden is vulnerable when channeling strong spells. Use these opportunities to unleash your most powerful strikes and inflict massive damage.

General Tips for Boss Battles

- Maintain Calm and Focus: Boss bouts may be fierce and difficult. Stay cool, concentrate on monitoring the boss's habits, and adjust your approach as appropriate.

- Experiment with Different Tactics: If one technique isn't working, don't be scared to try something different. Experiment with various weapons, skills, and strategies to see which works best on each boss.

- Practice Makes Perfect: Some bosses may need many tries to overcome. Use each try to learn more about the boss's habits and improve your approach. With practice and determination, you will finally triumph.

With these methods and ideas, you'll be well-prepared to face the tough bosses of Black Myth: Wukong. Each boss encounter tests your abilities and dedication, providing a gratifying challenge for those who are prepared. Accept the challenge and let your battle and tactical skills guide you to victory over these great opponents.

CHAPTER 6

Character Progression

In Black Myth: Wukong, your journey is as much about development and mastery as it is about adventure and fight. The way you develop Wukong's talents and manage your resources will have a huge influence on your overall game success. This chapter looks at how to improve Wukong's talents, create a strong skill set, and efficiently manage your critical resources.

Levelling Up: How to Improve Wukong's Abilities

As you go through Black Myth: Wukong, leveling up Wukong is critical for defeating more difficult adversaries and unlocking new powers. Leveling up is more than simply getting numerical numbers; it's about making smart decisions that fit your playstyle and goals.

To begin, accumulating experience points (XP) via battle, fulfilling missions, and discovering secret regions is critical. Each level increases your skill points, which may be used to improve certain talents and traits. Understanding how to appropriately distribute these points will significantly improve your entire gaming experience.

Focus on improving fundamental skills that suit your chosen battle style. If you like aggressive melee fighting, consider investing in talents that improve your physical assaults and defensive abilities. If you prefer a more magical approach, emphasize skills that improve your spellcasting and elemental capabilities.

Developing the Ultimate Skill Set

Developing the ideal skill set for Wukong requires a careful mix of offensive, defense, and utility. Your skill development decisions should reflect both the problems you confront and your unique playstyle.

Begin by examining your battle preferences and the sorts of foes you face the most. For example, if you are often confronted by huge groups of adversaries, investing in area-of-effect abilities and crowd control talents may be quite beneficial. These abilities may help you handle several adversaries more effectively and lessen the chance of being overwhelmed.

Alternatively, if you want a more targeted approach, look into talents that increase single-target damage and survival. Abilities that boost critical hit chances or grant temporary invincibility may change the course of a fight against more formidable opponents.

Furthermore, don't underestimate the value of utilitarian skills. Abilities that promote exploration, such as faster mobility or better navigation, may make your trip across the game's huge globe more fun and efficient.

Developing a diverse skill set is also important for adjusting to varied settings. As you meet different sorts of bosses and difficulties, possessing a diverse collection of skills will enable you to alter strategies and react successfully to new dangers.

Manage Resources: Health, Mana, and More

In Black Myth: Wukong, successful gameplay is built on effective resource management. Keeping track of your health, mana, and other vital resources might be the difference between success and failure in difficult battles.

In fight, health is your most important resource. Monitor your health bar on a regular basis and utilize healing items or skills intelligently to prevent running out of them at critical periods. It is critical to strike a balance between using healing resources and saving them for more difficult situations.

Mana, on the other hand, is required for casting spells and using special abilities. Efficiently managing your mana pool allows you to cast strong spells and abilities when required. Consider purchasing upgrades or equipment that improve your mana regeneration rate or lower the mana cost of your skills.

In addition to health and mana, additional resources like stamina and unique energy bars may come into play throughout the gameplay. Stamina influences your capacity to do activities like evading and running, although special energy bars may be needed to execute strong attacks or abilities. Managing these resources efficiently guarantees that you can perform optimally throughout combat and exploration.

Balancing Resource Management and Combat Strategy.

To balance resource management and battle tactics, consider the following approaches:

1. Preparation: Before beginning challenging fights or exploring new places, make sure you have a enough quantity of health and mana restoring consumables. Restocking at stores or discovering hidden caches may supply you with the resources you want for difficult confrontations.

2. Resource Conservation: Use your resources wisely. During protracted conflicts, concentrate on preserving mana for crucial skills and health for emergency scenarios. This technique guarantees that you are ready for unanticipated problems.

3. Strategic Use of skills: Utilize skills that spend resources in ways that compliment your battle plan. Consider saving strong spells or healing abilities for vital periods rather than activating them at the outset of a conflict.

4. Upgrading Gear: Provide equipment that improves resource management. Items that improve your health pool, speed up mana regeneration, or give passive resource recovery may help you stay successful in combat.

Embracing growth and adaptation.

As you move through Black Myth: Wukong, seize the chance to expand and adjust your gameplay. The game's dynamic nature implies that new difficulties will need developing tactics and talents. To remain ahead of the game, evaluate your progress on a regular basis and adapt your character growth and resource management.

To summarize, mastering character evolution in Black Myth: Wukong requires a combination of deliberate skill development, smart resource management, and flexibility. By improving Wukong's talents to match your playstyle, developing a flexible skill set, and properly managing essential resources, you'll be well-prepared to face the game's difficulties and have a satisfying voyage. Accept the path of evolution and become a genuine master of the mythological world.

CHAPTER 7

Advanced Tactics

In Black Myth: Wukong, being a genuine master of the game entails exploring sophisticated methods that go beyond the fundamentals. As you hone your talents and explore the depths of Wukong's powers, you'll find tactics and strategies that will take your gaming to the next level. This chapter will present you with professional insights into battle mastery, the art of shapeshifting, and how to adjust your methods to various playstyles.

Expert Tips for Combat Mastery

Combat in Black Myth: Wukong is an exciting and diverse experience. To succeed in combat, you must go beyond simple button-mashing and adopt a more strategic approach. Combat mastery requires an awareness of the complexities of time, placement, and the successful application of skills.

Begin by improving your sense of time. Many of the game's most difficult opponents and bosses have attack patterns that you can anticipate and counter. Learning how to timing your dodges and counters may swing the tide of combat in your favor. Pay great attention to visual and aural signals that suggest an enemy's impending strike or special attack.

Positioning is equally important. In chaotic fights, keeping the appropriate posture might be the difference between victory and loss. Use the environment to your advantage by positioning yourself to dodge assaults while remaining in range to deliver harm. Take use of lofty spots to improve your view point, or utilize cover to protect yourself from oncoming bullets.

Another important part of battle skill is the proper use of Wukong's powers. Experiment with different attack, spell, and special move combinations to determine the best successful techniques for various enemy kinds. Practice chaining skills to increase damage and create gaps in opponent defenses. Mastering these combos involves work, but the results are well worth it.

Shapeshifting: Using Wukong's Transformations

Shapeshifting is one of Wukong's most distinctive and formidable talents. This skill enables you to shift into a variety of forms, each with unique benefits and tactical uses. Understanding how to employ shapeshifting correctly will significantly improve your fighting effectiveness and adaptability.

Wukong's transformations may give major benefits in both battle and exploration. For example, shifting into a more agile shape may improve your movement and dodging skills, enabling you to avoid assaults more easily.

Adopting a more powerful form, on the other hand, might boost your damage output and defensive skills, making you more combat-ready.

Each metamorphosis has its unique set of powers and qualities. Acquaint yourself with these forms and their special benefits. Some transformations may give you increased strength, enabling you to penetrate opponent defenses or deliver huge damage. Others may provide you greater stealth qualities, allowing you to avoid adversaries or approach targets unnoticed.

Understanding when and how to flip between forms is essential for effective shapeshifting. In fight, analyze the enemy's strengths and weaknesses to decide which transformation will be most effective. For example, if you're up against a fully armored opponent, a form that boosts your physical strikes can be more successful. If you're fighting a bunch of foes, a form that boosts your area-of-effect powers might provide you a strategic edge.

Adapting Strategies to Different Playstyles

One of the most fascinating parts of Black Myth: Wukong is the option to tailor your strategy to your own playstyle. Whether you prefer a direct and aggressive approach or a more methodical and sneaky approach, adjusting your techniques to your playing style may make the game more fun and rewarding.

If you prefer a direct approach, work on developing a character that specializes in close-quarters fighting. Invest in talents and abilities that will boost your melee attacks, defense, and survival. Use Wukong's transformations to increase your attacking strength and put pressure on your opponents.

Those who want a more tactical approach should concentrate on ranged assaults, crowd management, and smart usage of abilities. Create a play style that stresses strategic placement, resource management, and effective spell and ability usage. Use Wukong's shapeshifting skills to adapt to diverse battle circumstances, rotating between forms to maximise your efficiency in each scenario.

Stealthy players may benefit from prioritizing skills that improve evasion and stealth. Use transformations and powers that enable you to travel unseen, avoid adversaries, or attack from the shadows. Create plans that stress hit-and-run techniques, enabling you to do damage while avoiding direct confrontations.

Adapting your methods also entails comprehending and reacting to the numerous obstacles posed by the game's opponents and bosses. Each opponent type and boss encounter may need a different strategy, so be ready to adapt your tactics depending on the individual challenges you face.

Combining advanced tactics for optimal performance.

To attain peak performance in Black Myth: Wukong, integrate these advanced strategies into a unified and successful strategy. Mastering fight timing, location, and ability utilization will improve your overall combat performance. Shapeshifting may give you with varied tools for dealing with a variety of scenarios. Adapting your methods to your playstyle and the individual problems you face will guarantee that you are ready for any hurdle.

Ultimately, mastering Black Myth: Wukong requires practice, experimentation, and a willingness to adapt. Accept the challenge, fine-tune your techniques, and keep trying new ideas as you move through the game. With perseverance and talent, you may become a genuine master of Wukong's mystical kingdom.

CHAPTER 8

Crafting and Resources

Crafting and resource management are essential components of Black Myth: Wukong's adventure through the fabled realm. Mastering these components of the game will greatly improve your character's powers and survivability. This chapter delves into the fundamentals of acquiring materials, upgrading weapons and armor, and effectively managing resources, allowing you to completely unleash the might of Wukong.

Gathering Materials and Crafting Essentials

Crafting in Black Myth: Wukong is more than just a way to upgrade your gear; it's an essential part of your experience. The process starts with acquiring resources, each of which plays an important part in making and improving your gear.

To begin, acquaint yourself with the various materials accessible in the game. These may vary from ordinary commodities like ores and plants to exotic components discovered in secret areas or dropped by formidable foes. Each resource has a specific function, whether it's for building new things, improving old gear, or producing consumables to help you in combat.

Exploration is essential for locating these minerals. Explore many landscapes, from thick woods to perilous dungeons, and keep a look out for resource nodes and secret caches. Pay attention to surrounding indications and hints that might lead you to valuable stuff. For example, luminous plants or strange rock formations are often indicators of the availability of important resources.

Once you have acquired enough resources, you may begin the making process. Crafting in Black Myth: Wukong entails mixing elements to make new items or improve old ones. Access the crafting menu to see possible recipes and determine the materials required for each item. Recipes might vary, so try several combinations to find the most effective upgrades.

Upgrade Weapons and Armor

Upgrading your weapons and armor is critical to retaining a competitive advantage against more stronger opponents. In Black Myth: Wukong, each upgrade not only improves the main qualities of your armor, but it also often grants extra benefits or unique effects.

To upgrade your weaponry, begin by determining which parts of your equipment need better. Whether it's boosting damage output, improving elemental effects, or introducing new abilities, each upgrade should be tailored to your fighting strategy and playstyle. For example, if you depend on strong melee attacks, prioritize upgrades that increase your weapon's attack power and critical hit probability.

Armor improvements are also vital for increasing your survival. Enhanced armor may provide enhanced protection, resistance to different elements, and mobility. Consider upgrading armor components to address particular weaknesses or to improve traits that support your overall strategy. For example, if you regularly take elemental damage, improving your armor with elemental resistances might give a big benefit.

Keep in mind that upgrading gear often requires a mix of resources, including uncommon components that might be difficult to get. Prioritize upgrading goods that provide the most substantial rewards at your current level in the game. As you go, hunt for additional resources and recipes to improve your gear and prepare for increasingly difficult tasks.

Efficient Resource Management

Efficient resource management is critical to getting the most out of your crafting and upgrading efforts. Balancing material consumption and inventory management may help you avoid shortages and be prepared for what comes next.

Begin by categorizing your inventory and identifying the resources you utilize the most often. Keep track of your vital supplies and avoid accumulating needless goods. This helps to keep your inventory organized and enables you to concentrate on obtaining and employing genuinely useful resources.

Create a method for managing consumables and crafting supplies. For example, if you often use healing potions or mana restoratives, make sure you always have a enough supply. Regularly make and refill these things to prevent running out during important periods.

In addition to consumables, manage your crafting and upgrade resources by periodically evaluating your inventory and determining what you have in excess. Excess materials may be used for improvements or crafting experiments, and any surplus can be traded or sold to merchants to get further resources.

Efficient resource management includes arranging your crafting and upgrading tasks. Avoid devoting significant resources to low-priority improvements or goods that do not correspond with your present objectives. Instead, concentrate on making and improving goods that are most beneficial to your gameplay and strategy.

Balancing crafting and combat.

Crafting and resource management are not stand-alone tasks; they should supplement your combat and exploration efforts. Balancing these variables guarantees that you are constantly prepared for the difficulties you confront while also maximizing your tools and resources.

During exploration, aggressively acquire materials and look for possibilities to create and improve equipment. Use the time between bouts to improve your equipment and prepare for future clashes. By including crafting and resource management into your gaming routine, you'll keep your competitive edge and improve your overall experience.

In conclusion, mastering crafting and resource management in Black Myth: Wukong is a combination of acquiring materials, upgrading gear, and managing resources effectively. Understanding the fundamentals of crafting, upgrading weapons and armor, and balancing resource management will prepare you to tackle the challenges of the fabled realm and completely unleash Wukong's strength. Accept these parts of the game to improve your experience and achieve success on your epic quest.

CHAPTER 9

Multiplayer and Community

In the rich world of Black Myth: Wukong, the multiplayer experience adds an exciting depth to your trip. Whether you're collaborating with friends or competing against other players, the game's multiplayer and community features provide a rich and entertaining experience. This chapter looks into cooperative and competitive modes, discusses how to engage with the Black

Myth community, and provides helpful advice for success in online play.

Co-operative and Competitive Modes

Black Myth: Wukong has a number of multiplayer modes meant to improve your gameplay experience. Whether you like cooperative play, where collaboration and strategy are essential, or competitive modes in which you compete against other players, there is something for everyone.

In cooperative modes, you and your friends may work together to complete difficult objectives and defeat formidable enemies. Cooperation is crucial in this situation; combining your skills, pooling resources, and formulating plans together may make even the most frightening issues bearable. Communication is essential in both modes—whether you're utilizing voice chat or in-game texting, clear and efficient communication may change the course of a fight. Plan your approach, assign responsibilities depending on each player's skills, and adjust your plan as necessary to overcome obstacles and accomplish your goals.

On the other hand, competitive modes in Black Myth: Wukong provide an exciting test of ability against other players. These modes, whether they include violent PvP (player vs player) fights or competitive tournaments, are intended to test your talents to the maximum. Success in competitive play requires not just mastery of your own character, but also knowledge of your opponents' strategies. Study their playstyles, adjust your plan as needed, and take advantage of any opportunity to outmaneuver and outfight your opponents.

Join the Black Myth Community

Engaging with the Black Myth community enhances your game experience and allows for cooperation and companionship. The Black Myth: Wukong community is vibrant and varied, with players that are passionate about the game and its vast environment.

Begin by looking through internet forums and social media groups devoted to Black Myth: Wukong. These sites are wonderful opportunities for connecting with other gamers, debating strategy, and exchanging experiences. Join discussions, ask questions, and share your thoughts to become an active part of the community.

Participating in community events and activities is another excellent method to get involved in the game's social side. Many communities organize events like challenge runs, competitions, and collaborative projects to bring participants together. Participating in these events may result in unique awards, new connections, and increased pleasure of the game.

Don't forget to look at fan-created content and resources. The community often creates guides, artwork, modifications, and other items that might improve your gaming experience. Whether you're seeking for ideas, inspiration, or simply some funny fan creations, this material might help you interact with the game and its community.

Tips for Online Play:

Understanding the game's fundamentals isn't enough to excel in online play, whether in cooperative or competitive mode. Here are some practical advice to help you get the most out of your multiplayer experience in Black Myth: Wukong.

1. Communication is Essential: In cooperative modes, excellent communication with your team may make a big impact. To assure success, share information about opponent locations, coordinate plans, and provide mutual assistance. In competitive modes, talk with your team to develop strategies and adjust your strategy as the game develops.

2. Understand Your function: In cooperative gaming, recognizing your function within the team is critical. Whether you're a frontline tank, a support character, or a damage dealer, concentrate on performing your duty to help your teammates. In competitive modes, be conscious of your character's strengths and limitations and choose your role depending on the team's requirements and your own abilities.

3. experience and Adapt: Online gaming, like any other talent, becomes better with experience. Spend time developing your skills, researching other tactics, and learning from your experiences. Be willing to adjust your strategies depending on the changing variables of each match or meeting.

4. Stay Informed: Keep track of game updates and changes. Patches, new content, and balancing changes may all effect gameplay, so being informed will allow you to alter your methods and stay competitive.

5. Connect with other players to create a network of friends and allies. Having a solid group of gamers to partner up with may improve your multiplayer experience while also providing vital support and friendship.

6. Respect and Sportsmanship: Whether you're working with people or competing against them, keeping a courteous and sportsmanlike demeanor is critical. Respect other players, avoid unpleasant conduct, and concentrate on having fun. A cheerful attitude may improve the overall experience for everyone involved.

Balancing Multiplayer and Solo Play.

While multiplayer modes provide exciting chances for cooperation and competitiveness, it's crucial to balance your time between online gaming and solitary excursions. Solo play enables you to explore the game at your own speed, delving into narratives and devising tactics without the strain of multiplayer dynamics. Solo play allows you to hone your abilities, accomplish objectives, and earn materials, which will improve your multiplayer experience.

In conclusion, the multiplayer and community features of Black Myth: Wukong enrich and enliven your game experience. Mastering cooperative and competitive modes, participating with the community, and implementing practical online play tips will allow you to fully appreciate the game's dynamic and social components. Whether you're building new alliances, battling against opponents, or just enjoying the company of other players, these factors will enhance your adventure through the magical land of Wukong.

CHAPTER 10

Troubleshooting and FAQs

Navigating the mystical realm of Black Myth: Wukong may be an amazing experience, but as with any sophisticated game, there will be problems and questions. Whether you're having technical problems, struggling with gameplay mechanics, or just searching for answers to frequent questions, this chapter is here to help you overcome challenges and improve your gaming experience. Here's a complete guide to solving common difficulties and answering commonly asked questions so that your trip through Wukong's realm is as seamless and pleasurable as possible.

Common Issues and Solutions

It might be irritating to encounter difficulties when playing Black Myth: Wukong, but the majority of them have simple fixes. Here are some of the most frequent difficulties that gamers encounter and how to overcome them:

1. Performance Problems

If you're experiencing lag, stuttering, or crashes, it's probably due to performance concerns. Begin by determining if your system fulfills the game's minimal or recommended requirements. Insufficient hardware might cause poor performance, therefore updating your PC or console may be essential.

For quick repairs, consider changing the game's graphical settings. Lowering options like resolution, texture quality, and effects might help improve performance. Ensure that your graphics drivers are up to current, since older drivers might create compatibility difficulties. If the crashes continue, check the integrity of the game files via the game launcher or platform, since damaged files might cause instability.

2. Connection Issues

Multiplayer modes and online features demand a consistent internet connection. If you are having problems connecting to servers or experiencing slowness when playing online, first check your internet connection. Restarting your router or modem may remedy temporary connection difficulties. In addition, make sure that no other programs or devices are taking too much bandwidth, which might interfere with your gaming experience.

If you are having problems connecting to certain servers or experiencing issues, please visit the game's official forums or support channels. Server maintenance or outages might sometimes disrupt connection, thus being updated about these issues can help you understand and fix connectivity difficulties.

3. Bugs in gameplay

Bugs and glitches are an undesirable aspect of many games. If you run across an issue that affects gameplay, consider restarting the game or reloading a previous save. Sometimes a quick restart might remedy small problems. If the issue continues, check for game updates or patches, since developers often resolve known flaws.

Report any persistent difficulties to the game's support staff. Providing specific details about the problem, including how to replicate it and any error messages, may assist developers in successfully addressing and resolving the issue.

4. Account and Login Issues

If you're having problems entering into your account or using online services, make sure you're using the right login information and that your account is in good standing. Check for any server outages or maintenance periods that may be impacting login functionality.

If you have forgotten your password or are having account troubles, use the account recovery instructions supplied by the game's support staff. To regain access, you will usually need to prove your identity and change your password.

Frequently Asked Questions.

Navigating the realm of Black Myth: Wukong poses several concerns, particularly for rookie players. Here are some of the most often asked questions to help you make the most of your adventure:

1. How can I get new powers and upgrades for Wukong?

To unlock new skills and upgrades in Black Myth: Wukong, players must proceed through the game's plot, complete objectives, and battle adversaries. Pay attention to critical milestones and plot events that unlock new skills. Explore the game's locations extensively, as hidden mysteries and side missions might lead to important upgrades and improvements.

2. What do I do if I am stuck on a challenging boss or quest?

If you find yourself stuck on a particularly difficult fight or quest, try changing your tactics or approach. Analyze the boss's attack patterns and vulnerabilities, then modify your strategy appropriately. Upgrade your equipment and use the most effective skills and items for the circumstances.

If you continue to struggle, seek help from online resources, forums, or the community. Other players have often had similar issues and may provide helpful advice and tactics. Don't be afraid to retry previous areas or grind for more experience and resources to improve your character.

3. How can I increase my performance in multiplayer mode?

Improving your performance in multiplayer games requires practice and smart thinking. Concentrate on learning your character's skills and identifying their strengths and weaknesses.

Communication with your teammates is essential, so coordinate strategy and assist one another throughout matches.

Study successful players' methods and playstyles to learn about effective approaches. Practice consistently and adjust your strategy depending on the changing dynamics of each match. Remember to remain calm and attentive, since having a good attitude will improve your entire performance.

4. Where can I learn more about planned changes and events?

To stay up to speed on impending updates and events, follow official game channels such as the game's website, social media accounts, and forums. Developers use these sites to announce new material, fixes, and community activities. Joining neighborhood organizations and receiving newsletters may also help you stay up to speed on the latest news and happenings.

5. What should I do if a technical problem persists after routine troubleshooting?

If a technical problem continues beyond typical troubleshooting procedures, please contact the game's support staff for help. Provide thorough details regarding the problem, such as error messages, system specs, and measures taken to remedy it. The support staff may provide tailored advice and solutions to more complicated or unusual technical issues.

6. How can I participate in the game's community and give feedback?

Contributing to the game's community and offering feedback are excellent ways to improve your experience and help the creators. Participate in forums, discuss your experiences, and provide constructive comments on game mechanics and additions. Participating in community events and conversations may also help you interact with other players and positively influence the game's growth.

In conclusion.

Troubleshooting and finding solutions to commonly asked topics are critical components in enjoying and mastering Black Myth: Wukong. Understanding typical difficulties and their answers allows you to tackle obstacles swiftly and get back to the adventure. This chapter will provide you with the information you need to handle the game's complexity, resulting in a seamless and entertaining voyage through Wukong's mythological universe. Whether you're troubleshooting technical issues or looking for gaming assistance, keep in mind that tenacity, resourcefulness, and participation in the game's community are essential for success.

CHAPTER 11

The Future of Black Myth: Wukong

Black Myth: Wukong continues to fascinate gamers with its intricate narrative and thrilling gameplay, but the adventure is far from done. The creators have exciting plans to grow and modify the game, adding new material and experiences to improve and enrich your journey through Wukong's mystical universe. In this chapter, we will look at planned upgrades and expansions, as well as what the future holds for this incredible game.

Upcoming Updates and Expansions

The universe of Black Myth: Wukong is slated to expand even more with a series of planned upgrades and expansions. These enhancements promise to provide new features, missions, and regions that will engage players deeper into the game's rich story and dynamic gameplay.

New narratives and missions are among the most highly anticipated upgrades. As the creators continue to expand the game's rich backstory and detailed storytelling, players can expect new narrative content that delves into previously unexplored areas of Wukong's mythos. Expect to meet new people, solve mysteries, and embark on epic journeys that add to the current narrative and provide exciting plot twists.

In addition to story expansions, upgrades will provide new places and settings to explore. These new places are intended to provide distinct challenges and rewards, reinforcing the spirit of adventure and discovery that distinguishes Black Myth: Wukong. From magnificent vistas to treacherous dungeons, each new location brings new experiences and chances for exploration.

The creators are also striving to improve gaming mechanics and features depending on user input. This involves fine-tuning battle systems, balancing gameplay features, and adding new powers and personalization choices. These enhancements seek to maintain the gaming experience tough and rewarding, ensuring that players remain interested and delighted.

What to Expect in the Future of the Game

Looking forward, Black Myth: Wukong will continue to evolve with various intriguing innovations. The future of the game promises to add richness and excitement to the realm of Wukong.

1. Expansive content and immersive experiences.

Future upgrades are anticipated to concentrate on growing the game's content to provide even more immersive experiences. This might include new narrative arcs delving further into Wukong's past and mythology, as well as extra side missions and activities that give players more opportunities to interact with the game environment. Expect excellent storyline, detailed world-building, and intriguing material to keep the experience interesting and fascinating.

2. Enhanced Multiplayer Features

Multiplayer modes will continue to expand, with upgrades and additions aimed at improving the game's social and competitive features. This may include new cooperative and competitive modes, more multiplayer content, and features that improve player communication and coordination. The idea is to create a lively and active community in which participants may interact, cooperate, and compete.

3. Continuous developer support and community engagement.

The creators are devoted to providing frequent updates and active participation with the Black Myth: Wukong player community. This involves responding to comments, resolving difficulties, and making changes based on player experiences. The objective is to create a dynamic and responsive game environment in which players may feel heard and respected.

4. Potential Collaborations and Crossovers.

As the game's popularity grows, there is potential for fascinating partnerships and crossovers with other games and media. These collaborations might result in additional content, special events, and one-of-a-kind experiences that combine the universe of Black Myth: Wukong with other well-known properties. Keep a look out for announcements and surprises that may add additional aspects to your trip.

5. Evolution of Game Mechanics and Technology.

Advancements in gaming technology and gameplay will also influence the development of Black Myth: Wukong. This might feature enhanced visuals, AI, and more advanced gaming mechanics. The objective is to constantly push the limits of what is possible, resulting in an ever more immersive and engaging experience.

Engaging with the Game's Future.

Connect with the game's official channels to remain up to speed on the newest developments and make the most of what's to come. Follow development announcements, engage in community conversations, and monitor changes to stay informed. Engaging with the community and being informed will improve your experience and prepare you to dig into new material as it becomes available.

Embrace the Journey

The future of Black Myth: Wukong is full with opportunities and excitement. As the game evolves, players can expect an ever-expanding universe full with new adventures, challenges, and possibilities. Embrace the trip and stay tuned for what comes next as the magical realm of Wukong unfolds.

To summarize, the future of Black Myth: Wukong is as exciting and compelling as the game itself. With regular updates, interesting expansions, and a dedication to improving the player experience, the quest is far from done. Whether you're looking forward to fresh material or exploring the newest features, Wukong's expanding universe promises to keep you interested and intrigued for years to come.

Conclusion

As you finish reading Unleash the Power of Wukong: A Black Myth: Wukong Game Guide and Strategy Book, take a moment to ponder on the magnificent adventure that awaits you in the mythological land of Wukong. From the rich tapestry of the game's narrative to the deep mechanics of battle and exploration, you now have the knowledge and methods to fully master this epic quest. But, before you get back into the game, let's take a time to enjoy your journey and prepare for the difficulties ahead.

Final Thoughts & Mastery Tips

Throughout this guide, we've gone over every aspect of Black Myth: Wukong, from understanding the tale of Sun Wukong and mastering battle techniques to delving into the deep nuances of character advancement and multiplayer gameplay. As you go on your trip, keep in mind that mastering the game is more than simply learning every trick and tip—it's about enjoying the ride, adjusting to difficulties, and immersing yourself in the rich universe created by the creators.

This guide emphasizes the significance of preparation and adaptation. The world of Wukong is wide and full of unexpected turns, so your ability to adapt to new circumstances will be critical to your success. Whether you're confronting a challenging boss, exploring unexplored territory, or fighting in multiplayer fights, adaptability and smart thinking will be your most valuable assets. Don't be hesitant to try new tactics, learn from each one, and improve your strategies as you go.

Mastery of Black Myth: Wukong also entails ongoing study and progress. The game is intended to challenge and interest players, and there is always something new to find. Stay interested and open to new experiences, whether it's discovering hidden mysteries, honing your fighting abilities, or taking part in community activities. The longer you play the game, the more you'll realize how deep and difficult it is.

One last recommendation for mastering the game is to remain involved in the community. The active player community in Black Myth: Wukong is a rich source of advice, tactics, and friendship. Connecting with other players, exchanging experiences, and engaging in debates will provide you with insights and help to improve your gaming and enrich your adventure.

Encouragement for your journey ahead

As you prepare to begin or resume your trip in Black Myth: Wukong, keep in mind that every great journey has trials, successes, and moments of discovery. Embrace every part of the game with excitement and interest. The world of Wukong is a rich and immersive experience, and every time spent exploring, fighting, and developing provides a chance to learn and grow.

It's easy to get caught up in the pursuit of perfection, but don't lose sight of the excitement of exploration and discovery. Enjoy the process of figuring out the game's tale, understanding its mechanics, and conquering its obstacles. Each triumph, no matter how minor, demonstrates your talent and devotion.

Remember, even the most experienced players began as beginners, and each player's path is unique. Do not get disheartened by failures or problems. Use them as an opportunity to learn, adapt, and grow. Your patience and commitment will result in achievement and mastery.

As you continue to explore the magical kingdom of Wukong, take pride in your accomplishments and talents. Celebrate your accomplishments, and keep moving ahead with confidence and excitement. The universe of Black Myth: Wukong is enormous and ever-changing, with more to explore and accomplish.

In conclusion, thank you for accompanying me on this adventure through Unleash the Power of Wukong: A Black Myth: Wukong Game Guide and Strategy Book. I hope this book has given you important insights, practical methods, and a greater respect for the game. May your journey through the magical kingdom of Wukong be full of excitement, difficulties, and successes. Accept the voyage ahead with enthusiasm and interest, and let the experience unfold.

Wukong's universe awaits you—dive in, explore, and use your power. Your journey is just starting.

APPENDICES

As you near the end of Unleash the Power of Wukong, it's time to dig into some important supplemental material that will enrich your experience in Black Myth: Wukong. The appendices in this book are intended to provide extensive tools for reaching mastery and increasing your relationship with the game. You'll discover a detailed look at the game's accomplishments and trophies, a dictionary of essential words and ideas, and other resources to help and improve your gaming. Let's look at these aspects and see how they might improve your experience.

Appendix A: Achievements and Trophies

In the fabled realm of Black Myth: Wukong, accomplishments and trophies are more than simply marks of success; they are milestones that represent your journey and commitment. This section contains a full list of all of the accomplishments and trophies available in the game, organized by category and difficulty. Each entry contains instructions for unlocking it as well as advice on how to achieve the desired rank.

From fighting legendary enemies to completing difficult tasks, accomplishments in Black Myth: Wukong are intended to both challenge and reward players. For example, mastering fighting methods or revealing hidden mysteries might result in important milestones that earn not just bragging rights but also substantial in-game prizes. This appendix explains out the prerequisites for each accomplishment, providing a clear path to follow.

Furthermore, recognizing these milestones might help you create objectives and plan your games. Whether you want to unlock every trophy or concentrate on certain achievements, this guide will help you monitor your progress and maximize your gaming experience. Each success demonstrates your ability and dedication, and this list will act as your key to unlocking every victory in the game.

Appendix B: A glossary of terms and concepts

Black Myth: Wukong is a game rich in mythology and mechanics, and navigating its dense universe requires a thorough comprehension of its own vocabulary and ideas. This glossary is a crucial reference tool for deciphering the game's language and developing a better understanding of its components.

This section defines and explains significant words, such as gameplay mechanics and character abilities, mythological allusions, and game-specific jargon. For example, if you come across terminology like "Celestial Energy" or "Demon Shapeshifting," this dictionary will give clarification and context. By becoming acquainted with these phrases, you'll be better prepared to face obstacles, comprehend game mechanics, and fully connect with the game's complex story.

A detailed dictionary not only improves your gaming but also increases your whole experience by ensuring you understand the game's terms. It bridges the gap between beginner and expert, making it simpler for you to interact with the game's more advanced aspects and techniques.

Appendix C contains additional resources and references.

To help you in your trip through the realm of Wukong, this appendix contains a handpicked collection of extra materials and references. These include official game websites, community forums, and other helpful resources that may help you understand and enjoy the game.

Here you'll find links to the game's official website, where you can keep up with the newest news and updates. Community forums and social media groups are available to let you interact with other players, share your experiences, and discuss strategy. There are also suggested strategy guides and walkthroughs to provide more insights and ideas.

Engaging with these tools helps you to remain up to date on game changes, have access to a multitude of player-generated information, and engage in debates that may provide fresh views and methods. They are essential resources for keeping in touch with the Black Myth: Wukong community and broadening your knowledge beyond the guide.

In conclusion,

The appendices in Unleash the Power of Wukong are designed to be your go-to resources for improving your gaming experience. This section is intended to help and empower you as you travel the legendary realm of Wukong by providing a complete list of accomplishments and trophies, a full lexicon of terminology and concepts, and other resources for continuing participation.

These appendices are intended not only to give necessary information, but also to increase your pleasure and mastery of the game. They are here to help you complete every milestone, explain every phrase, and link you to a larger community of gamers. As you begin your trip in Black Myth: Wukong, keep in mind that these tools are available to help you make the most of your experience.

Accept the difficulties, enjoy your accomplishments, and continue exploring the vast world of Wukong with the assurance that you have the skills and knowledge to succeed. Your journey is far from done, and with these appendices, you'll be well-equipped to discover every secret, complete every objective, and completely immerse yourself in the mystical land of Black Myth: Wukong.